Epitaphios

Epitaphios
Yiannis Ritsos

Smokestack Books
PO Box 408, Middlesbrough TS5 6WA
e-mail: info@smokestack-books.co.uk
www.smokestack-books.co.uk

Epitaphios
copyright the estate of Yiannis Ritsos, all rights reserved. Many thanks to
Eri Ritsou for permission to publish this translation of her father's work
Translation and Introduction copyright Rick M. Newton.

First published by Kedros, Athens 1936

ISBN 9780992740962

This book has been selected to receive financial assistance from English
PEN's 'PEN Translates!' programme, supported by Arts Council England.
English PEN exists to promote literature and our understanding of it, to
uphold writers' freedoms around the world, to campaign against the persecution and imprisonment of writers for stating their views, and to promote
the friendly co-operation of writers and the free exchange of ideas. www.englishpen.org

Smokestack Books is represented by Inpress Ltd

Introduction

Translator's Introduction

On May 10, 1936 Yiannis Ritsos saw a newspaper photograph of a woman mourning over the body of a dead youth in the street. The young man was her son, a worker in a tobacco factory in Thessaloniki, who had been killed by police during a march by strikers. Inspired by the picture, the 27-year-old poet composed a dirge which he imagined the mother singing. The resulting poem, published on May 12 in the Athens newspaper *Rizospastis (The Radical)*, consisted of 44 verses arranged in three sections. Titled *Moiroloi (Dirge)*, it was dedicated 'To the Heroic Labourers of Thessaloniki.

Later that year Ritsos revised and expanded the poem, renaming it *Epitaphios (Lamentation)*. It was composed of 224 verses in fourteen stanzas. Twenty years later, in 1956, he returned again to the piece and wrote an additional six stanzas (X-XV). The poem's final version, and the one printed and translated here, consists of twenty stanzas of eight rhymed couplets each (except for Stanzas XIX and XX, which contain nine couplets each).[1] In these 324 lines the poet transforms the original photograph into a universal image of human agony, resilience, and hope. As if he were heeding Aristotle's distinction between poetry and history, Ritsos presents a 'general and philosophic' lament, the sort of dirge any mother might sing over the body of her son.[2] In thus universalizing the mother's plight, the poet succeeds in speaking to the hearts of all people.

With the title *Epitaphios* the poet invites his audience to associate this lament with the ecclesiastical *Epitaphios Thrinos (Lamentation at the Tomb)*, the poetic dirge attributed to the Virgin Mary and other mourning women at the tomb of the crucified Christ. This traditional lament, based on early forms dating to the sixth century, is sung by entire congregations throughout Greece and all Greek Orthodox communities of the diaspora every spring during the Good Friday evening service.[3] It is traditional in many Greek villages for women, especially those who have lost loved ones, to keep a vigil inside the church at the end of the service and continue the dirge, singing laments from folk tradition as well as improvised verses of their own.[4] Ritsos points to this practice in the poem's brief prologue when he writes, 'She continues her lament.' The poet thereby reaches the broadest audience possible for a poet writing in Greek, for the *Epitaphios Thrinos* is known to nearly all speakers of the language: men and women, young and old, urban and rural, rich and poor, educated and uneducated, of all political persuasions.

The Greek populace's personal memories of the lament, furthermore, are inextricably intertwined with its context, since it is sung as part of an elaborate service which re-enacts the funeral of Christ and his descent into Hades. Wearing black in commemoration of the crucified Christ and their own dead, the faithful hold candles as they follow the funeral bier in an outdoor procession around the church.[5] The bier, a construction of intricately carved wood on four columns topped by a Byzantine dome and ornate with cut spring flowers filling every nook and cranny, contains a gold-and-crimson embroidered icon of the entombed Christ, which is also known as the *epitaphios*. This icon depicts the Virgin, surrounded by other mourning women, clutching the head of her dead son as she sings her lament. In many parts of Greece, the procession around the church expands into a procession through the streets of the entire neighborhood or town, the congregations of various parishes pouring on to the streets as they follow their own ornate bier. Onlookers from balconies participate by tossing flowers as the procession passes by, imitating the young girls who are stationed as 'myrrh-bearers' at the bier and sprinkle rose petals in its path. Ritsos evokes just such a procession in XIX.3, describing the funeral of the slain boy with, 'The balconies and markets roar, the streets narrow and wide, / While young girls pick spring flowers and strew petals on your hair.'

Upon re-entering the church, the congregation passes under the bier as it is held high over the doorway by young male pallbearers. This passage represents a spiritual renewal for all who participate: just as Christ passes beneath the earth in order to be reborn in the Resurrection, the faithful symbolically undergo a personal death and rebirth, stooping as they pass beneath the canopy and then standing straight as they re-enter the building.

The worshiper thus experiences genuine compassion (in the precise sense of the Greek-based word, 'sympathy') for Christ and all the dead. With the title *Epitaphios,* Ritsos evokes the traditional lament and the emotional, personal, and spiritual intensity with which it is associated.

Ritsos does not rely solely on the title, however, in order to call the *Epitaphios Thrinos* to the mind of his audience. The meter of the poem, fifteen-syllable lines arranged in couplets, is based on the meter of the traditional dirge. Likewise, many of the poem's images and motifs recall the Orthodox lament. In the ecclesiastical lamentation, for example, Christ is unjustly crucified between two thieves (St. I.8) and wrongly condemned (St. I.56), just as Ritsos' labourer is killed for demanding wages from 'men who were unjust' (XVI.1).[6] With his physical beauty Christ beautifies the natural world (St. I.9), just as the son in Ritsos' poem is handsome (III.1-5: VII.1; XIII.1-2; XV.1; XX.2), even erotically attractive (III.6-7), and lends his charms to make the world shine more radiantly in her eyes (VI.6-8; X.1-4). At the death of Christ, the sun quakes, draws in its light (St. II.52), sets, blackens, and dips beneath the earth (St. II.7, 30), just as in the modern poem all creation sets and the sun 'becomes a blackened ball' (XVII.1). Like the Virgin denouncing Judas (St. I.57, 61-63; St. II.51), the worker's grieving mother curses with even more vehemence the monstrous wolves who have shattered her son's fragile beauty (XX.5) and prays that they 'drown in all the blood' of their own slain parents and children (XVI.7).

Besides echoing the ecclesiastical lament, Ritsos employs themes and images which are found in dirges throughout the Greek literary tradition, ancient (*i.e.*, pre-Christian) and modern. In Homer, *Iliad* 22.79-89, for example, the aged Hecuba desperately attempts to dissuade Hector from confronting Achilles in a duel which she knows will end in her son's death. Wailing as if beating her breast in a premature dirge, she opens her bodice and pleads, 'Hector, my son, have mercy on these breasts and pity me, / if ever I held them out to you to soothe you in your pain.' Ritsos presents the identical image in his opening stanza: 'You do not speak, but look at me: I open up my blouse /And plunge my nails into the breasts that nursed you as a babe' (I.8). Also dating back to Homer is the tradition in which the bereft woman looks to the departed as the source and sole support of her entire life. In *Iliad* 6.428-429, Andromache invokes lamentation imagery when she pleads with Hector to remain within the walls of Troy and not venture into open battle. With all her relatives slain by Achilles, her husband is the only person left in her life: 'You are for me my father and my loving mother too. / You are, as well, my brother and my fine and stalwart spouse.' Ritsos' mourning mother echoes such a sentiment when she sings, 'When you stood tall, you seemed to me the father of the world' (X.4), and also when she says, 'You were the joy of my old age, my crowning pride, my rock' (II.1).

The extant corpus of Greek tragedy provides a range of motifs from which the poet freely draws. In Euripides' *Trojan Women* (1156-1206) Hecuba mourns the corpse of her grandson, Astyanax, whose broken body is carried into the theatre on Hector's shield. The old woman kneels over the tiny corpse and addresses it, part by part. She begins with the boy's head, fondling the ringlets of his hair. She then describes his face, kissed countless times by his mother. She kisses his lips, clasps his crushed hands, and concludes with the body *in toto* stretched out on the shield that serves as a coffin. The mother in Ritsos' poem follows a similar sequence in Stanza III. With a full couplet dedicated to each portion of her boy's body, she starts with his head and proceeds downward, dwelling on his curly hair, arched eyebrow, gleaming eyes, fragrant lips, broad chest, and sturdy thighs. She clutches his head, as is clear from I.6 ('I let my white hair down / And shroud the wilted lily of your fair and comely face') and XVII.5 ('Your breath's exhaling vapor, and I feel it on my cheek'). In XVI.6, she holds his crushed hands as if they were 'a pair of tiny birds, so crippled and in pain.'

Also prevalent in ancient tragic laments is the likening of the youthful departed, if unmarried, to a bride or groom. The mourning woman prepares the body for burial as if she were dressing her child for his or her wedding day. Within the genre of ancient tragedy, this macabre juxtaposition of wedding and funeral images heightens the tragic emotions of 'pity and fear,' as identified by Aristotle.[7] Thus, for example, in Euripides'

Medea (1024-1027) the deadly heroine of that play prepares to kill her two young sons and laments that she will never dress their marriage beds: as she envisions them in their pending death, she cannot avoid looking on them as grooms. Sophocles' *Antigone* (1155-1256) ends with the heroine's burial alive inside a rocky tomb, into which her fiancé rushes to kill himself, falling on her dead body as if it were their wedding night. Similarly, in Aeschylus' *Agamemnon* (1072-1330), the prophetess Cassandra, dressed as the bride of Apollo, suffers a violent death at the hands of Clytemnestra, who then displays the corpse, decked in its wedding attire, to the viewing audience.[8] Ritsos draws from this ancient tradition when his wailing mother declares (XVIII.5), 'This is no funeral service here: a wedding, more, it seems.' She laments that her son 'never stopped to take a wife or any girl's wealth' (VIII.4). Rather than enrich himself with a dowry, the young man gave away his riches of charm and compassion to others. As a small boy, the mother reminisces (X.1), he'd look out 'and through [his] eyes, the world gleamed, as at a wedding feast.' Looking on her son for the final time, she knows that she will never admire him as a bridegroom.

The blending of images from marriage and death also characterizes laments from modern Greek folk tradition. Sung, like Ritsos' poem, in fifteen-syllable couplets, many of these lamentations are interchangeable – with the alteration of a few words – with wedding songs. Charged with emotional intensity, both weddings and funerals mark the permanent departure of a loved one from the house.[9] These dirges, which Ritsos would have grown up hearing in his hometown of Monemvasia and the neighboring villages of the Peloponnese, stand as perhaps the strongest influence on his poem, accounting even for its initial title as simply, *Moiroloi (Dirge)*. In such folk laments it is common for the dead to be likened to a horseman among those on foot, a flower or grain of wheat withered before its time, a light that scatters the shadows, a tree providing protective shade, and a spring which flows generously with water for the thirsty.[10]

Such images fairly pervade Ritsos' poem. The mother sees her son as a horseman, for example, when she says, 'Ever the bright and shining knight, you always took the lead' (VIII.4). Flower and vegetative imagery mark such verses as 'the wilted lily of your fair and comely face' (I.6), 'Life's every flower I could see, but only through your eyes' (II.3), 'You were, my son, my fragrant grove with countless roots and leaves' (III.8), 'Let me thrive, my tall proud tree, in your protective shade' (VIII.3), 'My sturdy tree, my boy' (X.5), and 'My one and only flower' (XVI.5). The mother laments the loss of her light source when she cries, 'And now you're dead, your glow is gone. Our light has turned to dark' (VI.8), and when she laments, 'And so, my light, our window was a window on the world' (XV.3). The image of the gushing spring appears in negated form in such lines as 'the spring is parched and dry' (VIII.1) and 'O, how I wish I had the deathless water, a new soul' (XIX.1), referring to the folk tradition of the 'water of immortality' from which the dead might drink and return momentarily to life. In her despair, however, the mother knows that such beliefs are idle.

But perhaps the poet's most elaborate use of folk imagery is inspired by the Greek expression, *pouli mou* ('my bird'), a term of endearment with which mothers in Greece frequently address their male children. Within the context of this poem, the expression is especially apt. In the tradition of ancient tragedy, the departed is frequently likened to a young bird that has either flown prematurely from its nest or been stolen by predators, thereby driving the mother to screech as she searches in vain.[11] Thus, for example, in Sophocles' *Antigone* (423-428), the heroine discovers the unburied body of her brother lying on the open plain and 'cries out in the shrill keening of a mother bird that finds her nest bereft of its nestlings.' Honoring the two associations of this term with endearment and loss, Ritsos' crying mother addresses the boy from the outset as 'the nestling in my humble yard' (I.1). She finds the bird cage empty when she asks, 'Where is my boy? Where has he flown? Where has he fled and gone? / The cage has lost the bird it held' (VIII.1). She longed to keep him as her pet and feed him her life 'seed by seed' (VIII.2-3), and her weary glance would perch and rest on the arch of his slender eyebrow (III.2). He, in turn, looked on life as if it were a dove that needed only seeds from some open palm to stay alive (IX.5). But his murderers begrudged him even this much and, 'just like a flock of crows' (XVI.4), swooped down to silence him forever, leaving him with crippled wings that 'never more will fly' (XVI.6). The mother likewise finds her own 'wing broken and crushed' (XII.3), rendering her unable to lift herself from the street. 'Just like a brooding mother hen' (XIV.6), she would fuss and fret over her boy, but now that her joy 'has taken flight and fled' (XII.4), she asks eagles to give her 'claws and wings' (VII.8) with which to tear the heart of her enemies to shreds. The image comes full circle in the poem's closing line (XX.9), 'You, go to sleep, my bird,' echoing the opening image of the 'nestling in my humble yard' (I.1).

It is the physical and spiritual union of the mother with the son that gives the poem its deepest pathos. For at the outset she is stooped over the corpse, her body bent in grief, unable to part from it. Like the Virgin in the ecclesiastical lament, she cannot understand or accept that her child has died. The young worker's mother asks in disbelief, 'How can your eyes be shut so tight and you not see me sob?' (I.2). Such a line echoes the opening line of the Virgin's canonical lament: 'How can it be, O Life, that you are dead and dwell inside a tomb?' (St. I.1-2). The very phrase 'Life in the tomb' presents an oxymoron defying human comprehension. So strongly does the mother in Ritsos' poem identify with her child that she cannot imagine a situation in which he has no voice with which to speak, while she is left to 'ramble on with empty words of grief' (XII.8). Refusing to allow death to claim him, she calls on death to take her as well: 'If it's not possible to come back close to me, / Then take me with you, my sweet boy, and keep me company' (II.7). She repeats the wish in V.8: 'And I am waiting noon and night, my head and shoulders stooped. / Just for my darling, death, to come and take me to your side.'

In the Church's *Epitaphios Thrinos*, however, the Virgin utters no suicide wish, since she knows that her son will soon be resurrected.[12] The mother in Ritsos' poem, by contrast, takes it upon herself to raise the dead boy on the spot. Throughout the poem, she has one of only two choices if she is to remain resolved in never leaving his side: either she can die with him on the street or she can lift herself off the ground and, spiritually, take him with her. Abandoning her death wish by poem's end, she boldly opts for the latter, rising from her prostrate pose and standing straight: 'I straighten my bent body and I raise my fist up high. / Instead of tearing at my breasts – they're not to blame – I march' (XX.7-8). With this change of posture, the mother takes within herself the life that, up until this moment, has teemed inside her son. For he was the one who would stand tall and proud, rousing her adoration: 'When you stood tall, you seemed to me the father of the world' (X.4). But now the frail woman, 'the oldest of them all' (XX.4), stands up, fist in air, and takes to the streets.

Unlike the Virgin, therefore, who waits for the Resurrection which will take place 'on the third day' according to Biblical tradition, the mother of the slain labourer stands up on this very day and experiences – like the modern-day participants in the Good Friday service – a symbolic resurrection. In the end, she succeeds in preventing death from severing her from 'the child from her womb' (I.1), and positions herself to stand more closely to his side than she ever has before (XVIII.8). In fact, she avers that, 'You are not gone, my dear. You are right here inside my veins. / Go deep inside the veins, my boy, of everyone and live' (XX.1). She who once turned a deaf ear to his demands for social justice (XVIII.1) suddenly finds her heart opening up (XVIII.3) as she carries his message and voice to his comrades (XVII.8; XX.9). In the end, it is her mother's love that restores him to life: 'A thousand lives and more, my little bird, bind me to you, / And all who are loved never die, not even in their death' (XVIII.7).

Ritsos thus gives full poetic expression to the mother's despair and hope. The grieving woman confirms her belief that, even in the face of violent death, the living ingest the memory and voice of their dead and keep them alive. This belief in the paradoxical vitality of the dead is found elsewhere in Ritsos' poetry. In his *Eighteen Short Songs of the Bitter Motherland*, for example, the Greek spirit of *Romiosini,* suppressed by dictators, rises up in defiance and courageously harpoons the beast of oppression with the lance of the sun.[13] But the theme of the 'immortal dead' is not unique to this poet: it appears in the first formal literary expression of Greece's national identity.[14] In the *Ode to Liberty*, composed in couplets of rhyming fifteen-syllable lines and adopted as the Greek National Anthem, Dionysios Solomos (1798-1857) personifies Liberty as a corpse interred with the bones of the ancient Greeks. Her 'freedom-loving voice' waits patiently for the signal to return. Like the grieving mother in Ritsos' poem, Solomos' Liberty is initially bitter and withdrawn but ultimately returns with a fierce look in her eye. She rises from the sacred bones, swinging a frightening sword, while Ritsos' bereft mother picks up her son's rifle to stand up straight and march as she adds her own rage to that of his comrades (XX.9).[15]

In thus evoking literary traditions from Homer and Greek tragedy, the Byzantine *Epitaphios Thrinos*, secular funeral songs rich in folk imagery, and the message of the Greek National Anthem, Ritsos not only tugs at the heart strings of his audience but also rouses their spirit. On a metapoetic level, the poet may refer to the rousing effect of his own poem in the mother's description of her son's 'companions who'd stop by each evening to converse, / To talk and talk until their words would set them all ablaze, / And turn our house aglow with light, and all creation too' (V.6-7).

It comes as no surprise, therefore, that a poem which strikes so many chords in the Greek psyche has met with a strong and, at times, violent response. The politically conservative, indignant at the likening of a common labourer to a national hero and to Christ himself, branded the poem as subversive and blasphemous.[16] Shortly after its initial publication, the dictatorship of John Metaxas included the poem in a public book-burning ceremony in Athens at the Columns of Olympian Zeus, across from Syntagma Square. Twenty two years later, in 1958, the poem rose from the ashes, as it were, when composer Mikis Theodorakis wrote eight songs based on eleven of the twenty stanzas. He employed the rebetic dance rhythms of the slow *hassapiko*, fast *hassapiko*, and *zeimbekiko*, dances of the working urban class, and sent his score to the most prominent composer in Greece at the time, Manos Hadjidakis. Hadjidakis then set his colleague's composition in an arrangement of his own, suitable for a recital-hall performance before a seated audience. In 1960, he chose Nana Mouskouri, formally trained at the Athens Conservatory, to give the poem a lyrical and classical interpretation, to the accompaniment of guitars. At the same time, Theodorakis proceeded with his own arrangements as songs for dancing. He enlisted Manolis Hiotis for his pyrotechnic skill on the eight-string bouzouki and singer Grigoris Bithikotsis for his 'forceful, naturally vibrant voice.'[17] The bouzouki was, at that time, considered the instrument of taverns and hashish dens. Theodorakis incurred the charge of 'using beautiful poetry to cleanse a low and degrading musical instrument.'[18] Far from being discarded as trash for the fire, Ritsos' poem was now considered high poetry.[19]

Although the two musical versions of the *Epitaphios* have aroused much controversy and debate, it remains immaterial as to which interpretation is correct or 'better.' It is significant only that, with its distinctly Greek but also universal message, the poem can and does sustain such starkly different renditions. Some will therefore continue to regard Ritsos' poem as primarily a militant call to revolution penned by a communist, while others will hear it as a call to resurrection by a soulful poet.[20] These two readings, it goes without saying, need not be mutually exclusive. Indeed, the very genre of Greek lamentation poetry, rooted in antiquity and in modern folk tradition, is concomitantly literary and vernacular. As Ritsos himself stated in 1963, 'The language of poetry is one of synthesis, while that of criticism is one of analysis.'[21]

The poem became a slogan song of the Greek Left when, in May 1963, students gathered with Ritsos and Theodorakis outside a Thessaloniki hospital to mourn the assassination of parliamentary deputy Grigoris Lambrakis.[22] But in July 1984 Nana Mouskouri performed *Mera Magiou* ('One Day in May') from the poem's sixth stanza in a concert in the Herod Atticus Odeon in Athens, with Constantine Karamanlis, then President of the Third Hellenic Republic, in attendance. In the same recital, she performed works by Hadjidakis, Theodorakis, Bellini, Verdi, and Schubert. Though undeniably and unapologetically political in its inspiration and orientation, Ritsos' poem has achieved, over time, the status of a genuine classic, ultimately transcending the limitations of political affiliation and rising above the temporal events that inspired it. The now nearly eighty-year old composition is as fresh, poignant, and relevant as when it was first written.

A Note on the Translation

Some thirty years ago, to mark the fiftieth anniversary of the poem, which had never been translated into English, I published 'Ritsos' *Epitaphios*: Fifty Years Later' in *Journal of the Hellenic Diaspora* XIII.1-2 (1986) 5-51. Besides the poem, printed in a bilingual format with facing Greek and English texts, this thematic issue contained scholarly articles on the Fourth-of-August Regime of John Metaxas, in power at the time of the poem's initial publication. Because the journal's readership consisted largely of scholars and academic experts in modern Greek history, many of whom were readers of Greek, I opted for a close and literal translation, paying attention to the precise meaning of each word. The result, while exact in lexical explication, was in fact a work in prose. Observing line breaks that matched the breaks within and between Ritsos' original couplets, the translation 'had the 'look' of a poem but it 'read' as academic prose. It was a translation intended more for the reader than for the listener.

This translation, by contrast, is aimed for the ear, even as it attempts to retain fidelity to the sense of the Greek original. In particular, I have tried to capture the mostly iambic rhythm of Ritsos' poem with English iambs. Such a meter is as common in English-language verse as fifteen-syllable couplets are in modern Greek poetry. Iambs, which approximate the pattern of most spoken English, lend a natural sound to the mother's lament, thereby rendering it credible even in translation. The regular and repeating beat of the iamb, with its lub-DUB, lub-DUB rhythm, furthermore, is often associated in English with the beating of the heart. Thus, the iamb is both reflective of and compatible with the emotional state of the mother as she gives voice to her wide range of feelings.

Unlike Ritsos, however, I have opted for unrhymed couplets. My reasons are two. First, as a matter of personal taste, I find that English rhymes produce a trivializing effect in a protracted poem of 324 lines. This would be especially inappropriate in a dirge. Second, as a translator, I find that the need for consistent end-rhyme imposes severe limitations on English word choice, at times driving the translation-text far afield from the source-text, and at other times compelling the selection of a particular word or phrase that a mourning mother, however steeped in the rich tradition of Greek lamentation poetry, would be unlikely to utter in an English equivalent. The result would sound too much 'like a translation.' Rhyming would thus come only with a significant loss of fidelity to the original text and a compromising of the poem's credibility as a lament that a mother might actually sing.

The end result is an English poem in couplets of fourteen syllables per line. The first hemistich of each verse consists of an iambic tetrameter (*i.e.*, eight syllables), followed by a second hemistich of iambic trimeter (*i.e.*, six syllables). Honoring the line and couplet, rather than the individual word, as the unit of translation, I end each verse at the same spot as the poet. As in the Greek, the principal caesura falls, for the most part, after the eighth syllable, providing a brief pause just after the mid-point of the line and making the overall poem sound as if it were written in quatrains (such as Emily Dickinson's 'Because I Could Not Stop for Death'). Ritsos varies the rhythm in many parts of the poem by placing the caesura after the fourth or sixth syllable and also by placing more than one caesura within a verse (as in II.8, III.1, IV.6, IV.8, VII.6, VIII.1, VIII.8, XI.1, XI.4, XVII.6, XVIII.3, XIX.9, and XX.7). I have attempted to do likewise, where sense allows, since these intra-linear pauses vary the rhythm and prevent a sing-song effect from creeping in. Such caesurae, furthermore, lend a tone of naturally spoken language to the work, reflecting the mother's original discourse. Verses with multiple caesurae often have a staccato-like rhythm, reflecting the curt and frantic questions which the mother addresses to her non-responding son.

Finally, where Ritsos enjambs, running the syntax of one couplet into another (as in IV.5-6, V.6-7, VI.1-2, X.5-8, XII.1-3,

XIII.3-4, XIV.2-3, XVI.5-6, XVII.3-4, and XX.4-5), this translation follows suit. At such spots, the mother waxes lyrical, her emotions literally spilling over textual space into the next couplet. As in the original, however, even the enjambed couplets maintain both the meter and the syllable count. The final product, it is hoped, will leave the reader/listener with the impression that Ritsos' composition is a poem that lends itself to music precisely because it is poetic.

Rick M. Newton
Kent State University
August 2014

Notes

[1] See Pandelis Prevelakis, Ὁ Ποιητὴς Γιάννης Ρίτσος: Συνολικὴ Θεώρηση τοῦ Ἔργου του (Kedros Press, Athens 1983) 70-71.
[2] For this distinction between history, which deals with particular facts and events, and poetry, which aims for the universal and the philosophic, see Aristotle, *Poetics* 1451a 36-1451b 32 (= Chapter 9).
[3] See Margaret Alexiou, *The Ritual Lament in Greek Tradition: Second Edition, Revised by Dimitrios Yatromanolakis and Panagiotis Roilos* (Rowman and Littlefield Publishers, Inc., New York 2002) 62-78.
[4] See Prevelakis (above, note 1) 70 and Alexiou (above, note 3) 70.
[5] The Greek Orthodox tradition of mourning one's own dead at another's funeral reaches far back into pre-Christian antiquity. In Homer, *Iliad* 19.287-302, as the captive Briseis mourns the slain Patroclus, she invokes the memory of her dead father and brothers. The women around her 'joined in her lament for Patroclus, each one moved to recall her own dead.'
[6] For the purposes of this introduction, the abbreviation 'St.' refers to the Stasis (Roman numeral) and couplet (Arabic numeral) of the traditional *Epitaphios Thrinos*, as printed in the bilingual volume, Father George L. Papadeas, *Greek Orthodox Holy Week and Easter Services: A New English Translation* (Patmos Press, South Daytona, Florida 1996). The text of Ritsos' poem is referenced with Roman numerals (for the stanza, without the abbreviation, 'St.') followed by Arabic numerals (for the couplet).
[7] Aristotle, *Poetics* 1452a 2-1453b 36 (= Chapters 12-13).
[8] For a study of these and other passages from ancient tragedy, see Rush

Rehm, *Marriage to Death: The Conflation of Wedding and Funeral Rituals in Greek Tragedy* (Princeton University Press 1994). It is interesting to note, furthermore, that the conflation of wedding and funeral imagery marks the Greek Orthodox Church's so-called 'Bridegroom' services of Holy Week: Christ proceeds to his Passion as if he were a bridegroom.

9 See especially Loring M. Danforth and Alexander Tsiaras, *The Death Rituals of Rural Greece* (Princeton University Press 1982) 71-115.

10 For a survey of the allusions found in folk dirges, see Alexiou (above, note 3) 185-205.

11 The ancient association of the dead with birds is also evident in ancient Greek funerary art. See, for example, 'Grave Stele of a Little Girl' in Diana Buitron-Oliver, *The Greek Miracle: Classical Sculpture From the Dawn of Democracy, Fifth Century B.C.* (National Gallery of Art, Washington 1992) 141.

12 Earlier versions of the Virgin's Lament, such as Symeon Metaphrastes' tenth-century *Sanctae Mariae Planctus*, include expressions of a death wish. It is probable that the Orthodox Church's doctrinal stance against suicide discouraged such outbursts and expunged them from the final *Epitaphios Thrinos*: see Alexiou (above, note 3) 64-65.

13 See Yannis Ritsos, *Eighteen Short Songs of the Bitter Motherland, Translated by Amy Mims with Illustrations by the Poet* (Nostos Books, Minneapolis 1974). For a study of the resurrection theme as a constant in Ritsos' oeuvre, see George Pilitsis, 'Yannis Ritsos: A Poet of Resilience and Hope,' *Journal of Modern Hellenism* 17-18 (2000-2001) 91-105.

14 See Rick M. Newton, 'Yannis Ritsos: Poet of *Romiosini*,' *Journal of Modern Hellenism* 17-18 (2000-2001) 69-90.

15 In dedicating the original 'Dirge' 'to the heroic labourers of Thessaloniki,' Ritsos also invokes motifs from the traditional patriotic poems that celebrate the heroes of the 1821 Greek Revolution. His couplet in VI.1, 'One day in May I lost you, son, ... / In springtime,' not only invokes the paradox of springtime death but also brings to the audience's mind the martyrdom of the revolutionary hero Athanasios Diakos, impaled by Turks on April 24, 1821: 'Behold the season death has found to come here and to take me, / Now that the branches bloom with buds and grass sprouts from the ground.'

16 On the figure of Christ as a revolutionary hero in modern Greek poetry of the Left, see Prevelakis (above, note 1) 23-33.

17 According to Theodorakis, Bithikotsis had the 'forceful, natural vibrancy ... of a man who had suffered, even as the mother in the poem had suffered.' See George Giannaris, *Mikis Theodorakis: Music and Social Change* (Praeger Publishers 1972) 131.

18 See Giannaris (above, note 17) 133.

19 See Dimitris Papanikolaou, *Singing Poets: Literature and Popular Music*

in France and Greece (Legenda: Studies in Comparative Literature #11; Modern Humanities Research Association and Maney Publishing, Oxford 2007) 78-89. Papanikolaou suggests that the nearly simultaneous release (within two weeks of one another in the winter of 1960) of the recordings by Mouskouri and Bithikotsis was part of a commercial strategy by the recording companies of Fidelity and Columbia. He also suggests (pp. 70-78) that Theodorakis was striving, at the time, to develop a distinctively Greek form of 'popular' music (*laiko*) in response to Hadjidakis' endorsement of *rebetiko* as an esthetically valid, indeed spiritually profound, musical genre.

[20] See Prevelakis (above, note 1) 76.

[21] See Rick M. Newton, 'Yannis Ritsos: By Way of Introduction to the *Testimonies*,' *The Charioteer: An Annual Review of Modern Greek Culture* 29-30 (1987-1988) 111.

[22] See the introduction by Peter Bien in Nikos Stangos, translator, *Yannis Ritsos: Selected Poems* (Efstathiadis Group, Athens 1983) 23-25.

ΕΠΙΤΑΦΙΟΣ

Θεσσαλονίκη. Μάης τοῦ 1936. Μιὰ μάνα, καταμεσὶς τοῦ δρόμου, μοιρολογάει τὸ σκοτωμένο παιδί της. Γύρω της καὶ πάνω της, βουΐζουν καὶ σπάζουν τὰ κύματα τῶν διαδηλωτῶν – τῶν ἀπεργῶν καπνεργατῶν. Ἐκείνη συνεχίζει τὸ θρῆνο της:

I

Γιέ μου, σπλάχνο τῶν σπλάχνων μου, καρδούλα τῆς καρδιᾶς μου,
πουλάκι τῆς φτωχειᾶς αὐλῆς, ἀνθὲ τῆς ἐρημιᾶς μου,

Πῶς κλεῖσαν τὰ ματάκια σου καὶ δὲ θωρεῖς ποὺ κλαίω
καὶ δὲ σαλεύεις, δὲ γροικᾶς τὰ ποὺ πικρὰ σοῦ λέω;

Γιόκα μου, ἐσὺ ποὺ γιάτρευες κάθε παράπονό μου,
ποὺ μάντευες τί πέρναγε κάτου ἀπ' τὸ τσίνορό μου,

Τώρα δὲ μὲ παρηγορᾶς καὶ δὲ μοῦ βγάζεις ἄχνα
καὶ δὲ μαντεύεις τὶς πληγὲς ποὺ τρῶνε μου τὰ σπλάχνα;

Πουλί μου, ἐσὺ ποὺ μοὔφερνες νεράκι στὴν παλάμη
πῶς δὲ θωρεῖς ποὺ δέρνουμαι καὶ τρέμω σὰν καλάμι;

Στὴ στράτα ἐδῶ καταμεσὶς τ' ἄσπρα μαλλιά μου λύνω
καὶ σοῦ σκεπάζω τῆς μορφῆς τὸ μαραμένο κρίνο.

Φιλῶ τὸ παγωμένο σου χειλάκι ποὺ σωπαίνει
κ' εἶναι σὰ νὰ μοῦ θύμωσε καὶ σφαλιγμένο μένει.

Δὲ μοῦ μιλεῖς κ' ἡ δόλια ἐγὼ τὸν κόρφο, δές, ἀνοίγω
καὶ στὰ βυζιὰ ποὺ βύζαξες τὰ νύχια, γιέ μου, μπήγω.

Thessaloniki. May 1936. In the middle of the street a mother sings a dirge over her slain son. Waves of demonstrators – the striking tobacco workers – crash and resound around her. She continues her lament:

I

My son, the child from my womb, dear heart of my own heart,
The nestling in my humble yard, my desert's only bloom.

How can your eyes be shut so tight and you not see me sob?
Why don't you stir, why don't you hear the bitter words I cry?

My son, you'd cure my every grief and fill my every void.
You'd fathom every thought and fear that ranged beneath my brow.

But now, why don't you breathe a word? Why don't you comfort me?
Can't you divine the dreadful wounds devouring my heart?

You used to bring me water in the cupped palm of your hand.
Why can't you see me lashed about and trembling like a reed?

Here in the middle of the street I let my white hair down
And shroud the wilted lily of your fair and comely face.

To your sweet lip I give a kiss. It's ice-cold and dead still,
As if it were enraged with me, so firmly clenched and tight.

You do not speak, but look at me: I open up my blouse
And plunge my nails into the breasts that nursed you as a babe.

II

Κορώνα μου, ἀντιστύλι μου, χαρὰ τῶν γερατειῶ μου,
ἤλιε τῆς βαρυχειμωνιᾶς, λιγνοκυπαρισσό μου,

Πῶς μ' ἄφησες να σέρνουμαι καὶ νὰ πονῶ μονάχη
χωρὶς γουλιά, σταλιὰ νερὸ καὶ φῶς κι ἀνθὸ κι ἀστάχυ;

Μὲ τὰ ματάκια σου ἔβλεπα τῆς ζωῆς κάθε λουλούδι,
μὲ τὰ χειλάκια σου ἔλεγα τ' αὐγερινὸ τραγούδι.

Μὲ τὰ χεράκια σου τὰ δυό, τὰ χιλιοχαϊδεμένα,
ὅλη τὴ γῆς ἀγκάλιαζα κι ὅλ' εἴτανε γιὰ μένα.

Νιότη ἀπ' τὴ νιότη σου ἔπαιρνα κι ἀκόμη ἀχνογελοῦσα,
τὰ γερατειὰ δὲν τρόμαζα, τὸ θάνατο ἀψηφοῦσα.

Καὶ τώρα ποῦ θὰ κρατηθῶ, ποῦ θὰ σταθῶ, ποῦ θἄμπω,
ποὺ ἀπόμεινα ξερὸ δεντρὶ σὲ χιονισμένο κάμπο;

Γιέ μου, ἂν δὲ σοῦναι βολετὸ νἄρθεῖς ξανὰ σιμά μου,
πάρε μαζί σου ἐμένανε, γλυκειά μου συντροφιά μου.

Κι ἂν εἶν' τὰ πόδια μου λιγνά, μπορῶ νὰ πορπατήσω
κι ἂν κουραστεῖς, στὸν κόρφο μου, γλυκὰ θὰ σὲ κρατήσω.

II

You were the joy of my old age, my crowning pride, my rock,
My shining sun in winter's depth, my cypress slim and tall.

How can you leave me all alone to drag myself in pain,
Bereft of light, without a crumb, without a drop to sip?

Life's every flower I could see, but only through your eyes.
I'd greet each morning with a song, but only through your lips.

With your two arms, which I caressed a thousand times and more,
I held the earth in my embrace, and all the world was mine.

From your own youth I took my youth and chuckled to myself.
Old age evoked no dread in me. I disregarded death.

And now, what can I hold on to? Where can I go or stay?
I'm left alone, a withered tree, lost in a snowy plain.

My son, if it's not possible to come back close to me,
Then take me with you, my sweet boy, and keep me company.

Although my legs are weak and thin, I'll walk along your side.
And if you tire, I will clutch you sweetly to my breast.

III

Μαλλιὰ σγουρὰ ποὺ πάνω τους τὰ δάχτυλα περνοῦσα
τὶς νύχτες ποὺ κοιμόσουνα καὶ πλαϊ σου ξαγρυπνοῦσα,

Φρύδι μου, γαϊτανόφρυδο καὶ κοντυλογραμμένο,
– καμάρα ποὺ τὸ βλέμμα μου κούρνιαζε ἀναπαμένο,

Μάτια γλαρὰ ποὺ μέσα τους ἀντίφεγγαν τὰ μάκρη
πρωϊνοῦ οὐρανοῦ, καὶ πάσκιζα μὴν τὰ θαμπώσει δάκρυ,

Χείλι μου μοσκομύριστο ποὺ ὡς λάλαγες ἀνθίζαν
λιθάρια καὶ ξερόδεντρα κι ἀηδόνια φτερουγίζαν,

Στήθεια πλατειὰ σὰν τὰ στρωτὰ φτερούγια τῆς τρυγόνας
ποὺ πάνωθέ τους κόπαζε κ' ἡ πίκρα μου κι ὁ ἀγώνας,

Μπούτια γερὰ σὰν πέρδικες κλειστὲς στὰ παντελόνια
ποὺ οἱ κόρες τὰ καμάρωναν τὸ δείλι ἀπ' τὰ μπαλκόνια,

Και γώ, μὴ μοῦ βασκάνουνε, λεβέντη μου, τέτοιο ἄντρα,
σοῦ κρέμαγα τὸ φυλαχτὸ μὲ τὴ γαλάζια χάντρα,

Μυριόρριζο, μυριόφυλλο κ' εὐωδιαστό μου δάσο,
πῶς νὰ πιστέψω ἡ ἄμοιρη πὼς μπόραγε νὰ σὲ χάσω;

III

Your curly hair, through which I ran my fingers as you slept,
Those nights that I would lie awake and never leave your side.

Your eyebrow, smooth as braided silk, so finely drawn and thin,
The archway where my weary glance would perch and lightly rest.

Your gleaming eyes would catch the rays of morning's distant sky.
O, how I tried to fend them from a single dimming tear!

Your fragrant lips, whose very words made flowers sprout from stones,
Drove nightingales to spread their wings and withered trees to bloom.

Your broad chest, like a turtle dove's two smooth and outspread wings,
Brought calm and respite to my pain, and solace to my grief.

Your sturdy thighs, so tightly clad, admired by the girls
As they gazed from their balconies when you strolled by at dusk.

And I would hang a charm with a blue bead around your neck
To save you from the evil eye, my fair and fine young man.

You were, my son, my fragrant grove with countless roots and leaves.
I can't believe, in my ill fate, that you're now gone from me.

IV

Γιέ μου, ποιά Μοίρα στὄγραφε καὶ ποιά μοῦ τὄχε γράψει
τέτοιον καημό, τέτοια φωτιὰ στὰ στήθεια μου ν' ἀνάψει;

Πουρνὸ-πουρνὸ μοῦ ξύπνησες, μοῦ πλύθηκες, μοῦ ἐλούστης
πριχοῦ σημάνει τὴν αὐγὴ μακριὰ ὁ καμπανοκρούστης.

Κοίταες μὴν ἔφεξε συχνὰ - πυκνὰ ἀπ' τὸ παραθύρι
καὶ βιάζοσουν σὰ νἄτανε νὰ πᾶς σὲ πανηγύρι.

Εἶχες τὰ μάτια σκοτεινά, σφιγμένο τὸ σαγόνι
κ' εἴσουν στὴν τόλμη σου γλυκός, ταῦρος μαζὶ κι ἀηδόνι.

Καὶ γὼ ἡ φτώχεια κ' ἡ ἀνέμελη καὶ γὼ ἡ τρελλὴ κ' ἡ σκύλα,
σοὔψηνα τὸ φασκόμηλο κι ἀχνὴ ἡ ματιά μου ἐφίλα

Μιὰ - μιὰ τὶς χάρες σου, καλέ, καὶ τὸ λαμπρό σου θώρι
κι ἀγάλλομουν καὶ γέλαγα σὰν τρυφερούλα κόρη

Κι οὐδὲ κακόβαλα στιγμὴ κι οὐδ' ἔτρεξα ξοπίσω
τα στήθεια μου νὰ βάλω μπρὸς τὰ βόλια νὰ κρατήσω.

Κ' ἔφτασ' ἀργὰ κι, ὤ, ποὺ ποτὲς μὴν ἔφτανε τέτοια ὥρα
κι, ὤ, κάλλιο νὰ γκρεμίζονταν στὸ καύκαλό μου ἡ χώρα.

IV

What fate, my son, decreed for you, what fate decreed for me
That such a burning grief should rage so deeply in my breast?

You woke up early in the morn, you bathed and washed your hair
Before the far-off bell could toll the dawning of the day.

You kept on peering through the pane to catch the rising sun,
As if there were a festival and you might get there late.

There was a darkness in your eyes, a tightness in your jaw.
Your boldness made you look so sweet, both nightingale and bull.

And I, a fool without a care – how senseless could I be? –
Prepared your morning cup of sage and looked so lovingly

On all your charms, one at a time, my dear, and your bright face.
I giggled out of sheer delight just like a little girl.

Not for a moment did I fear or hasten from behind
To thrust my chest in front of yours to take the shots they fired.

I got there late. O, how I wish that hour had never come!
Would that, instead, the world's weight came crashing on my skull!

V

Σήκω, γλυκέ μου, ἀργήσαμε· ψηλώνει ὁ ἥλιος· ἔλα,
καὶ τὸ φαγάκι σου ἔρημο θὰ κρύωσε στὴν πιατέλα.

Ἡ μπλέ σου ἡ μπλούζα τῆς δουλειᾶς στὴν πόρτα κρεμασμένη
θὰ καρτεράει τὴ σάρκα σου τὴ μαρμαρογλυμμένη.

Θα καρτεράει τὸ κρύο νερὸ τὸ δροσερό σου στόμα,
θὰ καρτεράει τὰ χνῶτα σου τὸ ἀσβεστωμένο δῶμα.

Θὰ καρτεράει κ' ἡ γάτα μας στὰ πόδια σου νὰ παίξει
κι ὁ ἥλιος ἀργὸς θὰ καρτερᾶ στὰ μάτια σου νὰ φέξει.

Θὰ καρτεράει κ' ἡ ρούγα μας τ' ἁδρὸ περπάτημά σου
κ' οἱ γρίλλιες οἱ μισάνοιχτες τ' ἀηδονολάλημά σου.

Καὶ τὰ συντρόφια σου, καλέ, ποὺ τὶς βραδιὲς ἐρχόνταν
καὶ λέαν καὶ λέαν κι ἀπ' τὰ ἴδια τους τὰ λόγια ἐφλογιζόνταν

Καὶ μπάζανε στὸ σπίτι μας τὸ φῶς, τὴν πλάση ἀκέρια,
παιδί μου, θὰ σὲ καρτερᾶν νὰ κάνετε νυχτέρια.

Καὶ γὼ θὰ καρτεράω σκυφτὴ βραδὶ καὶ μεσημέρι
νἀρθεῖ ὁ καλός μου, ὁ θάνατος, κοντά σου νὰ μὲ φέρει.

V

Wake up, my son! It's late. Come now. The sun has risen high.
You haven't touched the plate I set. Your food is getting cold.

The blue work shirt you like to wear is hanging on the door
And waits for you to put it on your marble-sculpted skin.

A glass of cooling water waits for your refreshing mouth.
Our white-washed house waits patiently for you and your sweet breath.

Our cat awaits you just to play and frolic at your feet.
The sun has slowed its pace and waits to gleam within your eyes.

Our street awaits to see you and the long strides of your gait.
Our window slats are cocked to catch your nightingale voice.

Your comrades, who'd stop by the house each evening to converse,
To talk and talk until their words would set them all ablaze,

And turn our house aglow with light, and all creation too,
Will not set out for their night's work until you come back home.

And I am waiting noon and night, my head and shoulders stooped,
Just for my darling, death, to come and take me to your side.

VI

Μέρα Μαγιοῦ μοῦ μίσεψες, μέρα Μαγιοῦ σὲ χάνω,
ἄνοιξη, γιέ, ποὺ ἀγάπαγες κι ἀνέβαινες ἀπάνω

Στὸ λιακωτὸ καὶ κοίταζες καὶ δίχως νὰ χορταίνεις
ἄρμεγες μὲ τὰ μάτια σου τὸ φῶς τῆς οἰκουμένης

Καὶ μὲ τὸ δάχτυλο ἁπλωτὸ μοῦ τἄδειχνες ἕνα - ἕνα
τὰ ὅσα γλυκά, τὰ ὅσα καλὰ κι ἀχνὰ καὶ ροδισμένα

Καὶ μοῦδειχνες τὴ θάλασσα νὰ φέγγει πέρα, λάδι,
καὶ τὰ δεντρὰ καὶ τὰ βουνὰ στὸ γαλανὸ μαγνάδι

Καὶ τὰ μικρὰ καὶ τὰ φτωχά, πουλιά, μερμήγκια, θάμνα,
κι αὐτὲς τὶς διαμαντόπετρες ποὺ ἵδρωνε δίπλα ἡ στάμνα.

Μά, γιόκα μου, κι ἂν μοῦδειχνες τ' ἀστέρια καὶ τὰ πλάτια,
τἄβλεπα ἐγὼ πιὸ λαμπερὰ στὰ θαλασσιά σου μάτια.

Καὶ μοῦ ἱστοροῦσες μὲ φωνὴ γλυκειά, ζεστὴ κι ἀντρίκια
τόσα ὅσα μήτε τοῦ γιαλοῦ δὲ φτάνουν τὰ χαλίκια

Καὶ μοὔλεες, γιέ, πῶς ὅλ' αὐτὰ τὰ ὡραῖα θἄναι δικά μας,
καὶ τώρα ἐσβήστης κ' ἔσβησε τὸ φέγγος κ' ἡ φωτιά μας.

VI

One day in May I lost you, son, one day in May you left,
In springtime, when you'd go up on the terrace and look out,

And with your eyes you'd gaze and milk, until the final drop,
The light of all the universe and never take your fill,

And, with your finger pointed, you would show me one-by-one
All that was sweet, all that was good, all rosy-hued and soft.

You'd show the shining distant sea, as smooth and sleek as oil,
And all the mountains and the trees behind the azure veil,

The tiny humble creatures: all the birds, the ants, the shrubs,
Those diamond stones of water beading on the nearby jug.

But even as you showed me, son, the vastness of the stars,
I'd see them shine more brightly in the blue light of your eyes.

And in a voice so sweet, so warm, so manly you would speak
Of all the world's loveliness, like countless grains of sand,

And say that all this beauty that you saw was ours to keep,
And now you're dead. Your glow is gone. Our light has turned to dark.

.

VII

Εἴσουν καλὸς κ' εἴσουν γλυκὸς κ' εἶχες τὶς χάρες ὅλες,
ὅλα τὰ χάδια τοῦ ἀγεριοῦ, τοῦ κήπου ὅλες τὶς βιόλες.

Τὸ πόδι ἐλαφροπάτητο, σὰν τρυφερούλι ἐλάφι,
πάταγε τὸ κατώφλι μας κ' ἔλαμπε σὰ χρυσάφι.

Πῶς θὰ γυρίσω μοναχὴ στὸ ἐρμαδιακὸ καλύβι;
Ἔπεσε ἡ νύχτα στὴν αὐγὴ καὶ τὸ στρατὶ μοῦ κρύβει.

Ὤχ, δὲν ἀκούστηκε ποτὲς καὶ δὲ μπορεῖ νὰ γίνει
νὰ καίγουνται τὰ χείλια μου καὶ νἆμαι μπρὸς στὴν κρήνη,

Νἆμαι κοντά σου, ἀγόρι μου, καὶ νὰ σὲ κράζω, ὠϊμένα,
καὶ σὺ μήτε νὰ νοιάζεσαι γιὰ τὴ φτωχούλα ἐμένα.

Κανεὶς μὴ 'γγίξει ἀπάνω του, παιδί μου εἶναι δικό μου.
Σιωπή· σιωπή· κουράστηκε, κοιμᾶται τὸ μωρό μου.

Ποιός μοῦ τὸ πῆρε; Ποιός μπορεῖ νὰ μοῦ τὸ πάρει ἐμένα;
Ἄσπρισαν τὰ χειλάκια του, τὰ μάτια του κλεισμένα.

Δόστε μου, ἀϊτοί, νύχια, φτερὰ γιὰ νὰν τοὺς κυνηγήσω
καὶ τὴν καρδιά τους, μύγδαλο, νὰν τήνε ρουκανίσω.

VII

How good you were, how sweet and kind, with every charm and grace,
A garden full of violet blooms, as gentle as a breeze.

As if you were a tender fawn, your foot would nimbly step
Across the threshold of our house and give a golden glow.

How can I go back home alone to that abandoned hut?
The night has fallen on the dawn. I cannot see the street.

How can this be? Who ever heard of such a plight as this?
My lips are hot, aflame with thirst, right here before the spring!

And I, my boy, am at your side, as I cry out to you,
But you don't give a single thought to me in all my pain.

No one's to lay a hand on him! This child belongs to me!
He's tired now. Hush, all of you! He's fallen fast asleep.

Who's taken him away from me? Who could do such a thing?
His dear sweet lips have turned so white, his eyes so tightly shut!

O eagles, give me claws and wings so I can chase them down.
I long to tear their heart to bits and sliver it to shreds.

VIII

Ποῦ πέταξε τ' ἀγόρι μου; ποῦ πῆγε; ποῦ μ' ἀφήνει;
Χωρὶς πουλάκι τὸ κλουβί, χωρὶς νεράκι ἡ κρήνη.

Δὲν ἔμενες, καρδούλα μου, στ' ἄσπρο, μικρούλι σπίτι,
νὰ σ' ἔχω σὰν ἀφέντη μου, νὰ σ' ἔχω σὰ σπουργίτι,

Νὰ ταΐζω σε στὴ φούχτα μου σπυρὶ - σπυρὶ τὴ ζωή μου
καὶ μὲς στὸν ἴσκιο σου νὰ ζῶ, καμαρωτὸ δεντρί μου.

Καμιᾶς κοπέλας θησαυρὸ δὲ στάθηκες νὰ πάρεις·
ἔφευγες πάντα ἐμπρὸς λαμπρὸς καὶ πάντα καβαλλάρης.

Κ' εἶταν χαρά σου νὰ σκορπᾶς, καὶ δόξα σου νὰ παίρνουν,
ν' ἀνασηκώνεις ἀπ' τὴ γῆς τὰ ὅσα βογγοῦν καὶ γέρνουν.

Κι ὅλα τὰ πλούτια σου, γλυκέ, στὸν κόσμο ἐχάριζές τα
κι ὅλα τὰ χάρισες, κ' ἐμὲ μ' ἀφῆκες δίχως ζέστα.

Γιέ μου, δὲν ξέρω ἂν πρέπει μου νὰ σκύβω, νὰ σπαράζω,
γιά πρέπει μου ὄρθια νὰ σταθῶ, νὰ σὲ χιλιοδοξάζω.

Πότε τὶς χάρες σου, μιὰ - μιά, τὶς παίζω κομπολόϊ,
πότε ξανά, λυγμὸ - λυγμό, τὶς δένω μοιρολόϊ.

VIII

Where is my boy? Where has he flown? Where has he fled and gone?
The cage has lost the bird it held. The spring is parched and dry.

You would not stay, dear heart, inside our little white-washed home,
For me to keep you as my lord, to keep you as my pet,

To let me feed you, seed by seed, my life from my own hand
And let me thrive, my tall proud tree, in your protective shade.

You never stopped to take a wife or any girl's wealth,
Ever the bright and shining knight, you always took the lead.

It brought you joy to give away, that others might receive,
To raise up the downtrodden and to solace those in grief.

And all the riches that you had, you gave to all the world.
You gave them all away, my sweet, and left me in the cold.

My son, I don't know if I should stoop over you and mourn
Or if I should be standing proud to sing your boundless praise.

At times I fondle all your charms, like beads along a string,
At times I link them, sob-by-sob, into a doleful dirge.

IX

Ὤ, Παναγιά μου, ἂν εἴσουνα, καθὼς ἐγώ, μητέρα,
βοήθεια στὸ γιό μου θἄστελνες τὸν Ἄγγελο ἀπὸ πέρα.

Κι ἄχ, Θέ μου, Θέ μου, ἂν εἴσουν Θεὸς κι ἂν εἴμασταν παιδιά σου
θὰ πόναγες, καθὼς ἐγώ, τὰ δόλια πλάσματά σου.

Κι ἂν εἴσουν δίκαιος, δίκαια θὰ μοίραζες τὴν πλάση,
κάθε πουλί, κάθε παιδὶ νὰ φάει καὶ νὰ χορτάσει.

Γιέ μου, καλὰ μοῦ τἄλεγε τὸ γνωστικό σου ἀχείλι
κάθε φορὰ ποὺ ὁρμήνευε, κάθε φορὰ ποὺ ἐμίλει:

Ἐμεῖς ταγίζουμε τὴ ζωὴ στὸ χέρι: περιστέρι,
κ' ἐμεῖς οὔτ' ἕνα ψίχουλο δὲν ἔχουμε στὸ χέρι.

Ἐμεῖς κρατᾶμε ὅλη τὴ γῆς μὲς στ' ἀργασμένα μπράτσα
καὶ σκιάχτρα στέκουνται οἱ Θεοὶ κι ἀφέντη ἔχουνε φάτσα.

Ἄχ, γιέ μου, πιὰ δὲ μοὔμεινε καμιὰ χαρὰ καὶ πίστη,
καὶ τὸ χλωμὸ καὶ τὸ στερνὸ καντήλι μας ἐσβήστη.

Καί, τώρα, ἐπὰ σὲ ποιά φωτιὰ τὰ χέρια μου θ' ἀνοίγω,
τὰ παγωμένα χέρια μου νὰν τὰ ζεστάνω λίγο;

IX

All-Holy Virgin, if you were a mother just like me,
You would have sent your angel from beyond to help my son.

And if, O God, you were a God, and if we were your own,
You'd have compassion, as do I, on all your helpless flock.

And if you were both fair and just, you'd justly treat your world
For every bird and every child to have and eat his fill.

My son, the words you spoke were wise, your counsel sane and sage,
Each time that you would speak your mind, each time that you would say:

'It's we who feed the dove of life, straight from our open hand.
It's we who lack a single crumb to clutch within our palm.

'It's we who uphold all the earth on tough and weathered arms.
While gods above lord over us and menace with their scowls.'

No joy, my son, remains for me. My faith and trust are gone.
Our candle's dim and final light has flickered out and died.

And now, with cold and frozen hands, where will I find a flame
To spread my fingers just a bit and chase away this chill?

X

Ὅλα μοῦ τἄδειχνες ἐσύ, παιδί μου κι ἄρχοντά μου,
κι ὡς τἄβλεπες ὅλα ἔφεγγαν σὰ νἄταν ὥρα γάμου.

Κι ὅλα κοντά μου τἄφερνες, γνέφια, πουλιὰ κι ἀστέρια,
ποὔλεγα κ' ἔτσι νἄκανα θὰ τἄπιανα στὰ χέρια.

Καί, νάσου, ἕνα ἀνοιξιάτικο ποὐρχόταν συγνεφάκι
στὰ γόνατά σου νὰ τριφτεῖ σὰν ἄσπρο προβατάκι.

Κ' ἔτσι στητὸς μοῦ φαίνοσουν τοῦ κόσμου ὅλου πατέρας
καὶ πάλι τόσο ἀνάλαφρος σὰ φῶς καὶ σὰν ἀγέρας.

Καὶ κεῖ ποὺ σὲ καμάρωνα, πλατάνι, παλληκάρι,
ἔτρεμα μὴ πνοὴ ἀγεριοῦ στὸν οὐρανὸ σὲ πάρει,

Πάνου ἀπ' τὶς στέγες τῶν σπιτιῶν, πάνου ἀπ' τὰ δεντροκήπια
– χτύπος καρδιᾶς στῶν ἀστεριῶν τὰ πρῶτα καρδιοχτύπια –

Κεῖ πάνου ποὺ ἀχνοσβήνανε τοῦ σύθαμπου τὰ ρόδα
κι ἀνάμεσά τους βούλιαζε χρυσὴ τοῦ γήλιου ἡ ρόδα.

Κ' ἔτσι, πάει κ' ἔλα ἡ ὄψη σου, μιὰ φῶς, μιὰ σκιά, καλέ μου,
με ἴσκιωνε καὶ μὲ φώτιζε σὰ διάνεμα τοῦ ἀνέμου.

X

You showed me everything you saw, my little boy, my lord,
And through your eyes, the world gleamed, as at a wedding feast.

You brought it all so close to me – the clouds, the birds, the stars –
That all I had to do was reach and grab them with my hand.

Look here! A tiny springtime cloud that looked just like a lamb
Would come, all white, right up to you and rub against your knees.

When you stood tall, you seemed to me the father of the world,
And then you'd look as light as air, ethereal and bright.

And as I would admire you, my sturdy tree, my boy,
I'd tremble lest a breath of wind might waft you far away

Up to the sky and high above the rooftops and the trees,
– My heartbeat keeping time with the first heartbeat of the stars –

Up where the roses of the dusk would gently fade away,
While sun's gold orb would sink deep down and vanish in their midst.

And as your vision came and went, now bright, now dark, my dear,
It dappled me with shade and light, just like a fleeting breeze.

XI

Ἔτσι ἄχαρη, μὲ ὀμόρφαινες, κ' ἔτσι ἄμαθη – γιά κοίτα –
μὲς στὴ ματιά σου διάβαζα τῆς ζωῆς τὴν ἀλφαβήτα.

Καὶ μάθαινα ἀπὸ τὴν ἀρχή, πιὸ ὡραῖα, τὰ μαθημένα
καὶ μέτραγα στὰ δάχτυλα καὶ τἄβρισκα ὅλα ἕνα.

Ἕνα κ' ἡ γῆς καὶ ὁ οὐρανός, τὸ φῶς, τὸ χρῶμα, ἡ βιόλα
καὶ τοῦτο τὸ ἕνα εἴσουνα ἐσὺ καὶ πάλι ἐσύ 'σουν ὅλα.

Κ' ἔψαχνα ποῦ τὰ γνώρισα, ποῦ τἄϊδα, ποῦ καὶ πότες,
κ' ἔτσι σκυφτή, ὅπως τάϊζα ἕνα σούρουπο τὶς κόττες,

Ἔνιωθα πάνω μου βαθὺς ὁ θόλος ν' ἀνασαίνει
καὶ τ' ἄστρα ὡς νὰ μὲ χτένιζαν μὲ χρυσαφένιο χτένι,

Καὶ ξάφνου ἀνανοήθηκα τὸ τί 'ταν ἡ ἀναγάλλια
ποὺ μ' ἔπαιρνε καὶ μ' ἔφερνε στὰ οὐράνια ἀγάλια - ἀγάλια.

Κ' εἶδα τὸ πότε καὶ τὸ ποῦ, τὶς φωτοσκιὲς τοῦ δάσου: –
στὴν πόρτα ἐστέκοσουν ἐσὺ καὶ μ' ἔβλεπε ἡ ματιά σου.

Τώρα τὰ μάτια σου ἔκλεισαν καὶ γὼ κλείστηκα ἀπ' ἔξω
κι οὔτε ἔχω πέτρα νὰ σταθῶ καὶ δρόμο πιὰ νὰ τρέξω.

XI

I had no grace or charm – but look! – you made me beautiful.
I was unschooled, but in your eyes, I read life's alphabet.

And I would learn my lessons even better from the start,
By counting on my fingers and then adding up to one.

One was heaven plus the earth, plus light, plus hue, plus flower.
This single one again was you. You were my total sum.

And as the sun would set and I would stoop to feed my hens,
I wondered how I'd learned all this, and when I came to know.

I felt the sky's vast vault above, as it breathed in and out,
As if the stars, with golden comb, were stroking through my hair.

And suddenly I found the source of all this ecstasy
Transporting me to heaven's heights, ever so gradually.

And there I saw the when and where, the forest's speckled light:
And *you* were standing at the door, your gaze fixed firm on me.

But now your eyes have shut and I am locked outside the door.
I have no stone on which to stand or road on which to run.

XII

Γιέ μου, ἂν πονᾶς τὴν ὀρφανὴ ποὺ στέκει ἔξω ἀπ' τὴ θύρα,
ἄνοιξε τὰ ματάκια σου καὶ μιὰ στιγμούλα τήρα

Τούτη τὴ γριὰ τὴν ἄμοιρη, τὴ γριὰ τὴ διακονιάρα
π' οὔδε ἄνθρωπος κι οὔδε θεὸς τῆς ρίχνει μιὰ δεκάρα

Καὶ κάθεται καὶ μύρεται στὴ ματωμένη ρούγα
μὲ ξεγδαρμένη τὴν καρδιά, σπασμένη τὴ φτερούγα.

Γιέ μου, ὅλα κάνανε φτερὰ κι ὅλα μ' ἀφῆκαν πίσω,
δὲν ἔχω μάτι γιὰ νὰ δῶ, στόμα γιὰ νὰ μιλήσω,

Μόνο βαθιὰ κι ἀπόμακρα κάτι σὰ βουὴ διαβαίνει
κι ἀκούω τὴν ἴδια μου φωνὴ καὶ φαίνεταί μου ξένη,

Ξένη φωνή, πικρὴ φωνὴ – τί λέει καὶ ξαναλέει; –
καὶ κλαίω γιὰ σὲ καὶ κλαίω γι' αὐτὴ ποὺ τὴν ἀκούω νὰ κλαίει,

Καὶ χαίρουμαι νὰν τὴ γροικῶ, γιὰ ν' ἀνεβαίνει νάμα
πιὸ δυνατὸ ἀπ' τὴ ρίζα μου καὶ πιὸ στριγγὸ τὸ κλάμα.

Καὶ πάλι ἡ ἔρμη ντρέπουμαι, γιόκα μου, ἐσὺ νὰ λείπεις
κι ἀκόμα ἐγὼ νἄχω φωνὴ – ξόμπλι φτηνὸ τῆς λύπης.

XII

My son, if you have pity on this orphan at your door,
Just open up your eyes a bit and take a moment's look

At this old woman of ill fate, this beggar on the street
Who's never seen a single dime that God or man might toss,

Who sits and mourns along this road that's spattered with your blood,
Her heart inside now flayed and raw, her wing broken and crushed.

All that I ever had, my son, has taken flight and fled.
I have no eye with which to see, no mouth with which to speak.

But deep and distant, something like a cry now rises up.
It's my own voice I hear, but then, it doesn't sound like me.

A strange voice and a bitter voice, – I can't make out the words –
I cry for you. I cry for that poor woman as she sobs.

I'm glad to hear her, for it makes my own cry reach down deep
And well up from my very roots into a screeching howl.

But then again, it shames me, son, that you are gone from me
While with my voice I ramble on with empty words of grief.

XIII

Γιέ μου, τὸ στόμα σου καρδιά, τὸ φρύδι χελιδόνι,
τὸ μάτι δρόσο καὶ φωτιά, τανάλια τὸ σαγόνι.

Σὰν τὸ λιοντάρι δυνατός, κ' ἥμερος σὰν πιτσούνι
κ' ἡ ἀνάσα σου ὡς τ' ἀποσπερνὸ τοῦ κοπαδιοῦ κουδούνι.

Μὰ ὡς κάτι νὰ σὲ φώναζε μὲς στὴ χρυσὴν ἑσπέρα,
πάντα σου ἀγνάντευες ψηλὰ καὶ πάντα πάρα πέρα,

Σὰν κάποιος φίλος μπιστικὸς νὰ σφύραε, νὰ σ' ἐκάλει
γιὰ μιὰ κρυφὴν ἀντάμωση σ' ἀνέγνωρο ἀκρογιάλι.

Κ' ἔστηνα ἡ ἔρμη τ' αὐτὶ νὰ ἰδῶ, νὰ καταλάβω
τί σ' ἤθελαν καὶ τί 'θελες, σὲ ποιόνα ἔστριβες κάβο.

Κ' ἔψαχνα μὲ τὰ μάτια μου νὰ ἰδῶ ποῦ πάει ἡ ματιά σου
κι ὡς νἄνιωθες ποὺ ἀμίλητη σοὔκραζα 'γιέ μου, στάσου'

Γύρναγες, μ' ἀχνογέλαγες κ' ἔλεγες 'δῶ εἶμαι, μάνα'
κι' ἀκούγονταν ἀπόμακρα τοῦ ἑσπερινοῦ ἡ καμπάνα.

Κ' ἔπινα μὲ τὸ σάλιο μου μιᾶς τρυφεράδας γέψη
ποὺ ἐγὼ δὲ μάντευα καὶ σὺ τἄχες ὅλα μαντέψει.

XIII

Your mouth, my son, looks like a heart, your brow a winging bird,
Your eye refreshing dew and flame, your jaw as tight as pliers.

You're like a lion in your strength, as gentle as a dove.
Your breath soft like the evening bell of flocks returning home.

You always kept a lookout high and gazed out far and wide,
As if the evening's golden glow were calling out to you,

As if some loyal friend had, with a whistle, summoned you
To hold a meeting on some secret shore that you both knew.

And I, poor I, would cock my ear to eavesdrop and to learn
The cape that you were headed for and what you were about.

As with my eyes I'd search to see just where your eyes were fixed,
I spoke no words but you could hear me cry out, 'Wait, my boy!'

You'd chuckle at me, turn around, and say, 'Mother, I'm here,'
While chiming from afar I heard the church's vesper bell.

It brought a sweet taste to my mouth to marvel at just how
You'd read my every thought, while I could figure nothing out.

XIV

Ἄχ, γιέ μου, γιέ μου, γιόκα μου, δὲ δύναμαι ἄλλο ἡ ἔρμη,
χτυποῦν, χτυποῦν τὰ δόντια μου σὰ νὰ μὲ πιάνει θέρμη

Καὶ θέλω νὰ κουκουλωθῶ πιὸ πάνου ἀπ' τὸ κεφάλι
κι οὔδε ἥλιο πιὰ νὰ ματαϊδῶ, καὶ νά, πετιέμαι πάλι

Νὰ πῶ, νὰ πῶ τὶς χάρες σου, νὰν τὶς ξαναναστήσω,
σὰ νἆταν, γιέ μου, μπορετὸ νά σέ γυρίσω πίσω.

Γιατὶ ὅσο ἐδῶ εἰσουν, γιόκα μου, θάμπος βαθὺ μ' ἐκράτει
κ' ἡ σιγαλιὰ μὲ κλείδωνε σὲ μαγικὸ παλάτι.

Καὶ μόνο τὰ δυὸ μάτια μου σὲ παῖρναν τὸ κατόπι
σὰ δυὸ πιστὰ, πικρὰ σκυλιὰ ποὺ τἄσκιαξαν οἱ ἀνθρῶποι.

Καὶ σύναζα ὅλα σου βουβά, σὰν τὰ πουλιὰ μιὰ κλώσσα,
καὶ τώρα ποὺ μοῦ μίσεψες μοῦ λύθηκεν ἡ γλώσσα

Καὶ λέω καὶ λέω, ἀγόρι μου, δίχως νὰ ξαποστάσω,
σὰ νὰ κρατῶ ἕνα θησαυρὸ καὶ τρέμω μὴν τὸν χάσω.

Καὶ ν' ἀποθέσω θέλω τον στὰ γόνατα τῆς πλάσης
πιὸ πλούσια νὰ γενεῖ ἡ ζωὴ καὶ σὺ νὰ μὴ περάσεις.

XIV

My son, my son, my darling son, I can endure no more.
My teeth are throbbing, chattering. A fever's coming on.

I want to pull the blankets high and cover up my head.
I want to see the sun no more. But, look, I'm up again

To sing and sing of all your charms, to raise them from the dead,
As if it were within my strength to bring you back, my son.

Because, while you were here, a deep awe held me in its grip,
As if some spell of silence had been cast over my lips.

And just my eyes would follow you and trail from behind,
Like two scared dogs, their tails down, but loyal still to you.

Just like a brooding mother hen, I kept things to myself,
And now that you've abandoned me, my tongue has come untied.

I ramble on and on, my boy, and don't come up for air,
As if I clutched a treasure chest that might slip from my grasp.

I want to set it down upon the lap of all the world,
That life on earth might be enriched and you might never go.

XV

Στὸ παραθύρι στέκοσουν κ' οἱ δυνατές σου οἱ πλάτες
φράζαν ἀκέρια τὴ μπασιά, τὴ θάλασσα, τὶς τράτες

Κι ὁ ἴσκιος σου σὰν ἀρχάγγελος πλημμύριζε τὸ σπίτι
καὶ κεῖ στ' αὐτί σου σπίθιζε ἡ γαζία τοῦ ἀποσπερίτη.

Κ' εἶταν τὸ παραθύρι μας ἡ θύρα ὅλου τοῦ κόσμου
κ' ἔβγαζε στὸν παράδεισο ποὺ τ' ἄστρα ἀνθίζαν, φῶς μου.

Κι ὡς στέκοσουν καὶ κοίταζες τὸ λιόγερμα ν' ἀνάβει,
σὰν τιμονιέρης φάνταζες κ' ἡ κάμαρα καράβι.

Καὶ μὲς στὸ χλιὸ καὶ γαλανὸ τὸ ἀπόβραδο – ἔγια - λέσα –
μὲ ἀρμένιζες στὴ σιγαλιὰ τοῦ γαλαξία μέσα.

Καὶ τὸ καράβι βούλιαξε κ' ἔσπασε τὸ τιμόνι
καὶ στοῦ πελάγου τὸ βυθὸ πλανιέμαι τώρα μόνη

Κι ἀκόμα μήτε νὰ πνιγῶ, μήτε ν' ἀνέβω πάνω·
κάνω ἀπὸ κάπου νὰ πιαστῶ καὶ φύκι μόνο πιάνω.

Τὸ φύκι σπάει κι ὁ ὠκεανὸς μὲ σέρνει στὰ νερά του
κι οὐδὲ γνωρίζω τώρα ποιό τὸ πάνου, ποιό τὸ κάτου.

XV

You'd stand before the window, and your shoulders broad and wide
Would block the light and keep the sea and fishing boats from view.

Your shadow, like the archangel's, would flood throughout the house,
And twinkling in your ear I'd see the evening star's gold bud.

And so, my light, our window was a window on the world.
It looked out onto paradise, where all the stars would bloom.

And as you stood and gazed upon the sunset shining bright,
You looked just like a helmsman, and your room looked like a boat.

And in the evening's coolness, with its restful azure light,
We'd sail across the galaxy, inside its still and calm.

And then our boat went sinking down. The rudder broke in two,
And at the bottom of the sea, I'm floundering alone.

I've not yet drowned nor reached the top. I'm groping all about
For anything to hold on to, but seaweed's all I catch.

The seaweed breaks. The ocean pulls me far into its depths.
No longer can I tell which way is up, which way is down.

XVI

Τί ἔκανες, γιέ μου, ἐσὺ κακό; Γιὰ τοὺς δικούς σου κόπους
τὴν πλερωμή σου ζήτησες ἀπ' ἄδικους ἀνθρώπους.

Λίγο ψωμάκι ζήτησες καὶ σοὔδωκαν μαχαίρι,
τὸν ἵδρωτά σου ζήτησες καὶ σοὔκοψαν τὸ χέρι.

Δὲν εἴσουν ζήτουλας ἐσὺ νὰ πᾶς παρακαλιώντας,
μὲ τὴ γερή σου τὴν καρδιὰ πῆγες ὀρθοπατώντας

Καὶ χύμηξαν ἀπάνω σου τὰ σμουλωχτὰ κοράκια
καὶ σοὔπιαν τὸ αἷμα, γιόκα μου, σοῦ κλεῖσαν τὰ χειλάκια.

Τώρα οἱ παλάμες σου οἱ ἀχνές, μονάκριβέ μου κρίνε,
σὰ δυὸ πουλάκια ἀνήμπορα καὶ λυπημένα μοῦ εἶναι,

Ποὺ τὰ φτερά τους δίπλωσαν καὶ πιὰ δὲ φτερουγᾶνε
καὶ τὰ κρατάω στὰ χέρια μου καὶ δὲ μοῦ κελαϊδᾶνε.

Ὦ, γιέ μου, αὐτοὶ ποὺ σ' ἔσφαξαν σφαγμένα νὰν τὰ βροῦνε
τὰ τέκνα τους καὶ τοὺς γονιοὺς καὶ στὸ αἷμα νὰ πνιγοῦνε.

Καὶ στὸ αἷμα τους τὴ φούστα μου κόκκινη νὰν τὴ βάψω,
καὶ νὰ χορέψω. Ἄχ, γιόκα μου, δὲν πάει μου νὰ σὲ κλάψω.

XVI

My son, what wrong did you commit? From men who were unjust
You asked for payment in return for work that you had done.

You asked for a mere piece of bread, and they gave you the knife.
You wanted something for your sweat, and they cut off your hand.

You were no beggar pleading for a handout on the street.
With strength of heart you stood up tall and walked straight up to them.

And they swooped down upon you, son, just like a flock of crows
To drink your blood and silence you, to shut your mouth for good.

Your two hands now are drained of blood, my one and only flower,
Just like a pair of tiny birds, so crippled and in pain,

Who fold their wings for one last time and never more will fly:
I hold them now in my own hands, but they won't sing to me.

My son, I hope your slayers go back to their homes and find
Their children and their parents slain and drown in all the blood.

And in their blood I'll dye my skirt until it turns bright red,
And then I'll dance. O, son, my son, it's not right that I mourn.

XVII

Βασίλεψες, ἀστέρι μου, βασίλεψε ὅλη ἡ πλάση,
κι ὁ ἥλιος, κουβάρι ὁλόμαυρο, τὸ φέγγος του ἔχει μάσει.

Κόσμος περνᾶ καὶ μὲ σκουντᾶ, στρατὸς καὶ μὲ πατάει
κ' ἐμὲ τὸ μάτι οὐδὲ γυρνᾶ κι οὐδὲ σὲ παρατάει.

Καὶ δές, μ' ἀνασηκώνουνε· χιλιάδες γιοὺς ξανοίγω,
μά, γιόκα μου, ἀπ' τὸ πλάγι σου δὲ δύνουμαι νὰ φύγω.

Ὅμοια ὡς ἐσένα μοῦ μιλᾶν καὶ μὲ παρηγορᾶνε
καὶ τὴν τραγιάσκα σου ἔχουνε, τὰ ροῦχα σου φορᾶνε.

Τὴν ἄχνα ἀπ' τὴν ἀνάσα σου νιώθω στὸ μάγουλό μου,
ἄχ, κ' ἕνα φῶς, μεγάλο φῶς, στὸ βάθος πλέει τοῦ δρόμου.

Τὰ μάτια μου σκουπίζει τα μιὰ φωτεινὴ παλάμη,
ἄχ, κ' ἡ λαλιά σου, γιόκα μου, στὸ σπλάχνο μου ἔχει δράμει.

Καὶ νά ποὺ ἀνασηκώθηκα· τὸ πόδι στέκει ἀκόμα·
φῶς ἱλαρό, λεβέντη μου, μ' ἀνέβασε ἀπ' τὸ χῶμα.

Τώρα οἱ σημαῖες σὲ ντύσανε. Παιδί μου, ἐσύ, κοιμήσου,
καὶ γὼ τραβάω στ' ἀδέρφια σου καὶ παίρνω τὴ φωνή σου.

XVII

You've set, my star, and with you all creation too has set.
The sun's become a blackened ball and gathered in its glow.

The masses shove me as they pass. I'm trampled by the hordes.
But I don't budge. I hold my gaze unflinchingly on you.

They're picking me up from the ground. I now see countless sons.
But, my dear boy, I cannot bear to ever leave your side.

They talk to me the way you did. They try to comfort me.
They're wearing caps that look like yours. They're dressed the way you are.

Your breath's exhaling vapor, and I feel it on my cheek.
I see a huge light floating at the far end of the street.

The bright palm of some hand comes down and wipes away my tears,
And your dear voice, my son, has rushed and lodged within my soul.

And now that I am standing straight, my leg still bears my weight.
A gladsome light has lifted me, my boy, up from the ground.

Your body now is dressed in flags. You, go to sleep, my child,
While I head toward your brothers and I take your voice to them.

XVIII

Τὰ ποὔλεγες κι οὔτ' ἤθελα πιστέψω καὶ γροικήσω
κι ἀπόπαιρνά σε, μάτια μου, χωρὶς νὰ σὲ γνωρίσω,

Τὰ ποὺ δὲ μοῦπαν οἱ καιροὶ κι ὅλου τοῦ κόσμου οἱ γλῶσσες,
μοῦ τἄπε μόνο μιὰ στιγμή, ξεχωριστὴ στὶς τόσες.

Ποῦσαι, καλέ μου, νὰ χαρεῖς καὶ νὰ σταθεῖς κοντά μου;
Ἄκου, τὰ λόγια σου λαλῶ καὶ πλάτυνε ἡ καρδιά μου

Κι ὅλο τὸν κόσμο, σὰν κ' ἐσέ, δύνεται νὰ σφαλίσει
καὶ γέρεψε καὶ δύνεται νὰ πλάσει, νὰ γκρεμίσει.

Δὲν εἶναι ξόδι τοῦτο ἐδῶ, πιότερο γάμος μοιάζει,
δάκρυ καὶ γέλιο, ἀγάπη, ὀργή, τὸ κάθε μάτι στάζει.

Γιόκα μου, τὸ φρυδάκι σου τί σούφρωσες, γιά πέ μου,
μήπως κακοκαρδίστηκες ποὺ φεύγω σου, καλέ μου;

Πουλί μου, χίλιες δυὸ ζωὲς μὲ σένανε μὲ δένουν,
κι ὅσοι ἀγαπιοῦνται καὶ νεκροὶ ποτέ τους δὲν πεθαίνουν.

Κι ἂν δὲ λυγάω σὲ προσευχή, τὰ χέρια κι ἂν δὲν πλέκω,
γιέ μου, τὸ ξέρεις, πιὸ ἀπὸ πρὶν τώρα κοντά σου στέκω.

XVIII

I never wanted to believe or hear the words you'd say,
And I would chide you, my dear boy, and never understand.

But what the times and tongues of all the world never taught,
I've learned now in one moment that I never will forget.

Where are you now, my boy, to stand beside me and rejoice?
These are *your* words I'm saying. Hear? My heart has opened up

And now, like you, can take the whole wide world in its arms.
It's grown in might and has the strength to build up and tear down.

This is no funeral service here: a wedding, more, it seems,
As tears and laughter, love and rage, stream down from every eye.

Your brow, my boy, is furrowed. Tell me. What's the matter now?
Are you upset that I must go and leave you by yourself?

A thousand lives and more, my little bird, bind me to you,
And all who are loved never die, not even in their death.

And if I do not bow my head or fold my hands in prayer,
You know, my son, I've never stood more closely by your side.

XIX

Νἄχα τ' ἀθάνατο νερό, ψυχὴ καινούργια νἄχα,
νὰ σοὔδινα, νὰ ξύπναγες γιὰ μιὰ στιγμὴ μονάχα,

Νὰ δεῖς, νὰ πεῖς, νὰν τὸ χαρεῖς ἀκέριο τ' ὄνειρό σου
νὰ στέκεται ὁλοζώντανο κοντά σου στὸ πλευρό σου.

Βροντᾶνε στράτες κι ἀγορές, μπαλκόνια καὶ σοκάκια
καὶ σοῦ μαδᾶνε οἱ κορασιὲς λουλούδια στὰ μαλλάκια.

Γιὰ τὸ αἷμα ποὔβαψε τὴ γῆς ἀντρειεύτηκαν τὰ πλήθια,
– δάσα οἱ γροθιές, πέλαα οἱ κραυγές, βουνὰ οἱ καρδιές, τὰ στήθεια.

Ἔσμιξε ἡ μπλούζα τὸ χακί, φαντάρος τὸν ἐργάτη
κι ἀστράφτουν ὅλοι μιὰ καρδιὰ – βουλή, σφυγμὸς καὶ μάτι.

Ὤ, τί ὄμορφα σὰν σμίγουνε, σὰν ἀγαπιοῦνται οἱ ἀνθρῶποι,
φεγγοβολᾶνε οἱ οὐρανοί, μοσκοβολᾶνε οἱ τόποι.

Κι ὅπως περνᾶν, λεβέντηδες, γεροὶ κι ἀδερφωμένοι,
λέω καὶ θὰ καταχτήσουνε τὴ γῆς, τὴν οἰκουμένη.

Κ' οἱ λύκοι ἀποτραβήχτηκαν καὶ κρύφτηκαν στὴν τρούπα
– μαμούνια ποὺ τὰ σάρωσε βαρειὰ τοῦ ἐργάτη ἡ σκούπα.

Ὤ, ποῦσαι, γιόκα μου, νὰ δεῖς, πουλί, ν' ἀναγαλλιάσεις,
καί, πρὶν κινήσεις μοναχό, τὸν κόσμο ν' ἀγκαλιάσεις;

XIX

O, how I wish I had the deathless water, a new soul,
To give you and to wake you up for just one moment more,

For you to see your dream come true, to take joy and delight,
To see it standing next to you, complete and full of life.

The balconies and markets roar, the streets narrow and wide,
While young girls pick spring flowers and strew petals on your hair.

The crowds have grown courageous from the blood that's stained the earth –
With groves of fists and seas of shouts, high crests of hearts and chests.

The worker joins with soldier now, the khaki with the blue.
A single heart shines in them all – one will, one pulse, one gaze.

O, what a lovely sight it is when people join in love:
The skies above blaze with their light, the lands around smell sweet.

And as these young men make their way, strong in their brotherhood,
They look like they can take the world and all the universe.

The wolves have made a full retreat and slunk back to their holes,
Like ants swept up and whisked off by a common workman's broom.

Where are you, son, to see all this and revel in the sight?
Embrace the world before you leave. Then, take your lonely path.

XX

Γλυκέ μου, ἐσὺ δὲ χάθηκες, μέσα στὶς φλέβες μου εἶσαι.
Γιέ μου, στὶς φλέβες ὁλουνῶν, ἔμπα βαθιὰ καὶ ζῆσε.

Δές, πλάγι μου περνοῦν πολλοί, περνοῦν καβαλλαραῖοι, –
ὅλοι στητοὶ καὶ δυνατοὶ καὶ σὰν κ' ἐσένα ὡραῖοι.

Ἀνάμεσά τους, γιόκα μου, θωρῶ σε ἀναστημένο, –
τὸ θώρι σου στὸ θώρι τους μυριοζωγραφισμένο.

Καὶ γὼ ἡ φτωχὴ καὶ γὼ ἡ λιγνή, μεγάλη μέσα σ' ὅλους,
μὲ τὰ μεγάλα νύχια μου κόβω τὴ γῆ σὲ σβώλους

Καὶ τοὺς πετάω κατάμουτρα στοὺς λύκους καὶ στ' ἀγρίμια
ποὺ μοὔκαναν τῆς ὄψης σου τὸ κρούσταλλο συντρίμμια.

Κι ἀκολουθᾶς καὶ σὺ νεκρός, κι ὁ κόμπος τοῦ λυγμοῦ μας
δένεται κόμπος τοῦ σκοινιοῦ γιὰ τὸ λαιμὸ τοῦ ὀχτροῦ μας.

Κι ὡς τὄθελες (ὡς τὄλεγες τὰ βράδια μὲ τὸ λύχνο)
ἀσκώνω τὸ σκεβρὸ κορμὶ καὶ τὴ γροθιά μου δείχνω.

Κι ἀντὶς τ' ἄφταιγα στήθεια μου νὰ γδέρνω, δές, βαδίζω
καὶ πίσω ἀπὸ τὰ δάκρυα μου τὸν ἥλιον ἀντικρύζω.

Γιέ μου, στ' ἀδέρφια σου τραβῶ καὶ σμίγω τὴν ὀργή μου,
σοῦ πῆρα τὸ ντουφέκι σου· κοιμήσου, ἐσύ, πουλί μου.

XX

You are not gone, my dear. You are right here inside my veins.
Go deep inside the veins, my boy, of everyone and live.

The marching crowds are passing by, on horseback and on foot.
Just look at them: they're tall and strong, as beautiful as you.

And in their midst, I see you resurrected, my dear son,
Your face painted a thousand times on each and every one.

And I, the poor and frail one, the oldest of them all,
Stoop down and, with my nails, tear the soil into clods

And throw them straight into the face of all those monstrous wolves
Who took your fragile beauty, son, and shattered it to bits.

And you, a corpse, follow along. A knot swells in our throat
And turns into the noose we tie around the killers' necks.

And, as you wished (and as you'd tell me on those lamp-lit nights),
I straighten my bent body and I raise my fist up high.

Instead of tearing at my breasts – they're not to blame – I march,
And through the veil of my tears I now discern the sun.

I'm heading for your brothers as I add my rage to theirs.
I've taken up your rifle, dear. You, go to sleep, my bird.